The Trinity
&
The Ministry

Michelline Jacquelle Porter

RWG Publishing
PO Box 596
Litchfield, IL 62056
https://rwgpublishing.com/

Published in the United States of America

Paperback: 978-1-68411-988-2

So gather as a miracle is presented.

For "she" - as well - is bright to open life's expectancies.

The Trinity

And with crowning, I am washed with heart felt
pain and joy!

My cells are excited!

I glow!

I am becoming more sensible.

I prepare to make my own footprints.

Each day is lucrative for some thing!

Even if so, just rest...

In this new day, logarithms are my incentive.

With abundance, I can afford.

I am new – a supplanter.

And unto this earth, I shall till.

My wealth is noticeable!

I am now recognizable!

From the wilderness, I return.

I am made prepared for selection.

I follow well - the laws of nature.

Where there is new age, there is new order.

For we withhold phylogeny in our biology.

My domain is still.

And Held so; by divine authority.

In this order, I stand alone.

And presented onward:

The gift of abundance.

Thereupon I build for KINGDOM.

As Man is governed by his version of time,

we may continue through pace.

For we are subject to the tides.

A new era approaches.

An Aquarian is seen before his Age

And upon his head, I witness, a mortal wound -
though healed.

As *he* may be exceedingly strong.

And with him, I obtain one cycle and adjustment.

And then I may decipher a new way. .

I am sent ahead.

And I travel onward with 11-woman veterans.
And Beyond coincidence they are named so:
Michelle and Michelle and Magdalene and Marie
and Melissa and so forth and myself.

I am familiarized with various territories.

And there is acceptance of strengths and skills.

As I may be challenged of my knowledge and discernment of various perceptions and interpretations.

I recollect.

There is comfort in covenant.

A band of colors is displayed conveniently within my view, a spectrum within my reach - as a ribbon doorway that has touched down and centered upon me,

to greet me – with time.

An affirmation of protection.

And presented:

A Bachelorette of a New Order.

And here I stand – still as sand.

Now, I am up for Review.

I live, and therefore I learn:

My CREATOR

Shines the Fire that engages energies

Shifts Seed with wind

Drops the water which dampens soil

Withholds the root into the Earth

This GREATNESS, I adhere to.

For I follow *this* unyielding doctrine.

And stepping forward ...

I obtain reference, strategy, education,

Profession, government amenities and Ministry.

The Ministry

How do you remain grounded within your "self" even when approached by temptation?

____

____

____

____

____

____

____

____

____

____

**** Be still to gather concepts that are sensible.**

We know to be sensible as we are bound by a much greater existence.

How do *you* maintain a spiritual balance?

____

____

____

____

____

____

____

____

**** Be rewarded to weigh your options.**

WE are faced with choices that may compromise our future feelings of self.

How do you make well determined decisions?

____

____

____

____

____

____

____

____

****Explore avenues that are beneficial to your future.**

With life, there are demands.

How do *you* manage *your* concerns?

____

____

____

____

____

____

____

____

____

****Be guided to bend at knee as preparing to lift grand weight - even spiritual.**

Education is direction with the freedom to explore and discover.

What ways do *you* learn best?

____

____

____

____

____

____

____

____

****Ensure understanding by asking the right questions.**

WE are influenced by one another each day.

How do *you* practice discernment?

____

____

____

____

____

____

____

____

**** May we love by choice.**

Your *work* may be driven by your passion.

How do you avoid becoming overwhelmed during assignment?

____

____

____

____

____

____

____

____

____

**** Work as *you* are able.**

Your home influences your well being.

How do you introduce a positive atmosphere into *your* home and your surroundings?

____

____

____

____

____

____

____

____

**** Humor softens the soul.**

We confide in emotional security.

How do *you* determine sense of belonging when feeling unwelcomed and rejected?

____

____

____

____

____

____

____

____

____

**** Rediscover self-worth for fulfillment of your purpose.**

It is best to quickly release negative energy.

How do you divert your attention to a more positive source?

____

____

____

____

____

____

____

**** Life has no boundary on discovery.**

In order to endure obstacles, we require an amount of strength and skills.

How do you prepare for obstacles that you are to face?

____

____

____

____

____

____

____

____

**** Stamina withholds endurance.**

Intimacy allows an emotional connection to PEERS.

How do you maintain your relationships?

____

____

____

____

____

____

____

____

**** Communication ensures a desire to understand.**

It is subservient to love our neighbor.

In what ways do you benefit your community?

****Be an apostle of your community.**

Prayer allows us to reflect on situations through meditation.

How do *you* determine when it is necessary to reflect?

____

____

____

____

____

____

____

____

** When times are troubled, we must reflect.

Ancestral strength pushes us forward.

How do you navigate your intended path?

____

____

____

____

____

____

____

____

**** We are granted the freedom to span and orient for what is euphoric.**

Nourishment influences our well-being.

What diet is beneficial for your health?

** Harvest and be supplied with fruit and grain.

Recovery is a process that allows one to become full of the spirit.

How do you overcome negative attachments and addictions?

____

____

____

____

____

____

____

____

**** You may grow as you choose to release and grasp another concept.**

The quality of the spiritual environment impacts spiritual health.

In what ways do you impact life around you?

____

____

____

____

____

____

____

____

****Devotion allows us to maintain a positive attachment to the spirit.**

Rest is essential for well being.

How do you manage your rest periods?

____

____

____

____

____

____

____

____

**** Rest allows the body a moment to metabolize nutrients and rejuvenate.**

There is a discipline within you and within society.

How does your community provide guidance for the youth and care for the elderly?

____

____

____

____

____

____

____

**** It is reasonable to accept what is to be protected.**

Through works we establish roles.

How do you determine your placement while accepting the placement of others?

____

____

____

____

____

____

____

**** Employ your strengths.**

Development is influenced by social and environmental cues.

How do you maintain and govern your body?

____

____

____

____

____

____

____

____

____

____

**** We are prone to be sensible of areas such as of the eyes, neck, hands, sternum, spine, stomas, kidneys, gentiles, thighs, kneecaps, ankles, or feet.**

We must be calm to be still.

What Relaxation techniques work best for you?

____

____

____

____

____

____

____

____

**** As you focus, you may receive clarity.**

We are governed to receive order through Framework.

How do you adjust and adapt?

____

____

____

____

____

____

____

____

____

**** Familiarity increases recognition.**

We choose to implement as we are provided with sticks and stones.

How do you perform with quality?

____

____

____

____

____

____

____

** Sort, port, organize and release words and works in which you convey.

Discipline provides protective environment while influencing growth.

How would you define your Quality of Protection?

____

____

____

____

____

____

____

****Safe bonds and secure unions enhance life.**

Follow by way of direction.

Life sustains through optimal conditions -

Fulfilling the laws of nature.

Trust in the Equations of higher power.

Endure phases, Passovers, and

New light.

Be disciplined through balance, and

seek interest.

The Trinity
&
The Ministry

www.ingramcontent.com/pod-product-compliance
Lightning Source LLC
Chambersburg PA
CBHW051747050726
47598CB00003B/1365